UNIX:

Operating System Success in a Day

By Sam Key

Beginners Guide to Fast, Easy and Efficient Learning of UNIX Operating Systems!

2nd Edition

UNIX: Operating System Success in a Day

Table of Contents

Introduction

I want to thank you and congratulate you for purchasing the book, *"UNIX Operating System Success in a Day: Beginners Guide to Fast, Easy and Efficient Learning of UNIX Operating Systems!"*

This book contains proven steps and strategies on how UNIX is essential to your career.

In case that you are aspiring to be a programmer, learning UNIX is essential for you. UNIX is one of the key factors that revolutionized computers. If ever UNIX was not developed, it is possible that computers will be dedicated for work alone; programs will be crappier than they are, and the internet will regress a few years back. That is how UNIX is essential to the development of the computing industry.

On the other hand, if you are just curious about UNIX in general, then go ahead and read this book. The book will introduce you briefly on the world of operating systems and history of UNIX. Aside from that, the book will give you an idea on how UNIX is related to the most popular operating systems nowadays such as Microsoft Windows, Mac OS X, and Linux.

For programmers, you will understand how important UNIX is to your career. This book will give you a heads up on why you should study it and how it will benefit you. In addition, this book will let you understand why you do not have a clue about it in the first place.

Not only that, this ebook would also show you detailed guides on how to use UNIX, including how to start programs, open and transfer files, as well as how to make, open, and make changes to directories. You would even learn about handy UNIX utilities.

Thanks again for purchasing this book, I hope you enjoy it!

Part 1:

All about UNIX

Chapter 1: Operating System

An operating system is a set of programs or software that handles hardware and as well as other software. You can think of it as a program that bridges the gap between you, your programs, and the computer hardware. Most programs or applications usually rely on the operating system to run.

Operating systems handle all the necessary processes in order to make a computer operational. It usually handles the input and output of data. Also, it prepares data from input and output for both the computer and the user.

Most electronic devices with multiple functions have operating systems in them. A few of those devices are smartphones, smart televisions, gaming consoles, watches, and even refrigerators.

Some of the operating systems that you might already heard about are Microsoft Windows, Mac OSX, iOS, Android, and Linux (together with its multiple distros). Some of the operating systems that you might not be familiar with are Chrome OS, BSD, Solaris, HP-UX, and UNIX.

The main component of the operating system is the kernel. The kernel is the one that handles the computer's memory, CPU, storage, and other devices. Mostly, it acts like a traffic enforcer that controls how resources are handled and used in the computer.

On the other hand, the kernel and the operating system play a huge role in managing the computer's memory (RAM) and CPU usage. A lot of problems will occur if programs are allowed to dictate or control their resources.

For example, a program may use the memory located at one part of the RAM. Without the kernel, another program may overwrite the data placed on that part of the RAM. And if that happens, the program that needed the overwritten data may crash.

UNIX: Operating System Success in a Day

Aside from that, the kernel makes it easier for developers to create programs. Instead of writing everything from scratch, some of the most basic functions that a program needs are already in the operating system and the kernel.

In some cases, the programmer only needs to worry about how he can communicate to the kernel in order to get what he wants in his program. Most of the time, developers really do not need to think about that.

Those are just few of the responsibilities of the operating system's kernel. On the other hand, the operating system also handles the computer's security, networking, and user interface.

Another component of the operating system is the shell. The shell is where the users and the operating system interact. And lastly, the operating system comes with utilities. They are small essential programs that make the operating system useable by itself and the computer.

Without operating systems, computer programs will be required to be built from ground up. Also, it will be difficult for programs to work with each other. And making the program compatible with other programs is a tough job for a developer.

On the other hand, operating systems make it easier for regular computer users to interact with the computer. Also, with the bundle of tools and programs in operating systems, it is much easier for the layman to maintain and use a computer.

Chapter 2: What Is UNIX?

UNIX is an operating system that was developed by AT&T in 1970. It was created in Bell Labs research center (Bell Laboratories). Now, Unix refers to as a family of operating systems that support multiuser and multitasking features — features that were considered huge leaps in computation back then.

Originally, UNIX systems were designed for programmers. It was supposed to be used for workstations that were dedicated to software development. It was mostly used in laboratories, universities, and research facilities.

The main goal of having UNIX is to have a portable, multiuser, and multitasking system. The main characteristics that defined UNIX back then are its plethora of small programmed tools and its behavior towards files and devices.

Despite being obscured by most modern operating system nowadays, UNIX has been one of the biggest innovators in operating system development. During its time, UNIX was the first operating system that was written using a high level language (C to be precise). Back then, developers had this belief that operating systems should be written using assembly language, which was rather difficult, time consuming, and delimiting.

One of the influences it made in modern operating systems is its hierarchical file system. While UNIX users were able to enjoy easier file management thanks to nested subdirectories, devices treated as files, and files being treated as simple byte arrays, its contemporaries were limited to one-level deep directories and divided storage devices.

Another thing that made UNIX indispensable and became popular in the world of operating systems is its ability to be installed and used in inexpensive systems and almost every platform. Back then, computers that were sold came with a preinstalled operating system.

Buyers were stuck with what they will get. For example, if you buy an IBM computer back then, you will be stuck with IBM's OS. Thanks to UNIX, cross platform standardization emerged.

On the other hand, the UNIX operating system is not the only one that influenced the world of programming. Its developers have created an impact, too. A few of the things that UNIX developers were able to impart in computing, or program development in general, are the worse is better development style, 17 UNIX rules, and the UNIX philosophy.

The only problem with UNIX systems is that they are proprietary. Unfortunately, this can be easily ignored back then when other operating systems and system unites were pricy and UNIX systems were relatively inexpensive. However, nowadays, everybody can get operating systems free of charge and those operating systems are capable of matching the standards of UNIX.

Chapter 3: Spawns of UNIX

It can be safely said that UNIX did not only influence modern operating systems, but it also became the template or the model of the new operating systems to come. You might know it, but most of the popular operating systems today are based on UNIX.

Modern versions of UNIX (or are licensed by the Open Group to use the UNIX brand) today are Apple's A/UX, OS X, and iOS; HP's (Compaq and DEC) Tru64 and HP-UX; Oracle's (Sun) Solaris; SGI's (Silicon Graphics Inc.) IRIX; and IBM's AIX. Of all the UNIX variants listed, Apple's OS X enjoys the most attention and popularity.

Why is OS X more known than the other UNIX operating systems? First of all, the market for OS X and other UNIX operating systems listed previously differs. OS X and iOS are marketed towards regular consumers — unsophisticated computer users. On the other hand, other UNIX operating systems are marketed towards enterprises. Most UNIX based operating systems are dominant in internet servers.

UNIX Like

On the other hand, there is Linux. Unlike Mac OS X, Linux is not fully recognized as UNIX by some operating system experts and program developer because it is not certified under the Single UNIX Specification.

However, Linux developers consider UNIX as its root. After all, the Linux kernel, which is the core component of the Linux operating system, was designed after UNIX. It is compliant of POSIX (Portable Operating System Interface). And due to that, Linux was branded as a UNIX like system.

UNIX as Number One Operating System

For a while now, many media and news sites have hailed UNIX as the number one operating system in the world. Most people would have sworn that Microsoft Windows is the number one operating system. They are actually right — if they are talking about desktops and laptops. It might not be the most popular, but it is the most used — even if people have no idea what it is.

Take note that computers are not the only devices that require and use operating system. Devices such as smartphones, tablets, watches, and even cars do have operating systems, too. And if you lump all those devices together, desktop computers will be outnumbered fast.

UNIX being the number one operating system is caused by the surge of people buying devices with operating systems. The number of smartphones alone can overwhelm the number of computers that were bought and are still being used. Unfortunately, Microsoft's operating system has a small market share in the mobile industry.

Well, UNIX being the most popular operating system today is mostly thanks to Linux, Android, OS X, and iOS. It is even ironic that people do not even know UNIX in the first place. Most people will even say question how Android OS and iOS are related. They cannot be UNIX, right? What is UNIX in the first place? Well, it is amusing to think that UNIX is the most popular operating system, but it is one of the most obscured as well.

Chapter 4: The Fall of UNIX to Obscurity

Back then, UNIX seemed to be the greatest operating system. It has brought up multitudes of innovations in the computing scene. And it might have been incomparable to other operating systems. Unfortunately, its reign eventually ended.

During its time, many computers would rather have UNIX than any other computer with a different operating system. UNIX units were easier to use. They were relatively cheaper. They were easier to access and portable. And even today, most people who have used UNIX and other operating systems on the market would rather use UNIX based operating systems.

But what exactly happened? Why was the name UNIX forgotten or why did it disappear in the minds of many? It is even unfortunate that when a person says UNIX, there will be a certain individual that will walk towards that guy and will ask him, "Do you mean Linux?"

Price – yes, it was all about pricing. UNIX faced its downfall when personal computers or PCs became available on the market. Despite the PC's limitations compared to proprietary computer systems back then, it was favored by the masses. After all, regular consumers do not need to worry about performance as long as they can use their computer for typing text, saving files, sending e-mails, playing games, and managing spreadsheets.

Unfortunately, a relatively new operating system that would disrupt the market for computers entered the fray. And that was Microsoft Windows. Unlike UNIX, Microsoft Windows is a whole lot cheaper and it was compatible with the cheap PC.

Despite being less complex and useful than UNIX, Microsoft Windows was able to win the hearts of many computer users. And even though programmers were in favor of UNIX, they needed to get Windows. After all, creating programs for the Windows system became an attractive and profitable venture due to its fast growing user base.

Software developers were not the only people who were shifting to the new operating system, but hardware manufacturers followed suit in order to take advantage of the PC and Windows partnership.

And that is just a small part of the story. If you would think about it, UNIX was greater in every aspect. However, why would UNIX be defeated by a mediocre— which was how developers saw it back then — operating system? There were speculations on who or what to blame. Unfortunately, those speculations were right on the spot.

AT&T's mismanagement over UNIX was to blame. AT&T had full control over UNIX back then. However, it became laid back in a sense despite the market for computers have shifted greatly towards the unsophisticated users. The company failed to cater to the needs of the market. It focused on serving the professionals. Most UNIX developers believed that if a person cannot remember and use commands, he does not need to use a computer.

For them, professionals were the only ones who needed computers and computers were not suited to be used at home. They did not know what a layman would do with a computer. After all, it was perceived that computers were made for work — not for personal use.

That was the largest hindsight that people working on UNIX encountered. In their defense, it did not matter if they did not make UNIX useable for regular people. They were right after all. UNIX was still the best when it comes to enterprise level computing.

However, it only made UNIX exclusive for the ones who use and know it. Time passed and UNIX was forgotten. The younger generations of programmers, developers, and normal computer users thought that the only operating systems out there were Microsoft Windows. Even Mac OS was unknown to the masses and was only known to elite people who can buy a Mac. And even Linux sounded foreign for regular consumers.

Chapter 5: UNIX versus Linux

During the time Windows was gaining a huge market share, UNIX, being the most popular operating system at the time, could have been saved and maintained if only Linux was released to the public a few years earlier. But what is Linux anyway? And how was it created and how is it related to UNIX?

Linux is a UNIX like operating system and is compliant to POSIX. Linus Torvalds created Linux and it was based of MINIX, which stands for mini UNIX. MINIX was created for educational purposes; however, it offers a lot of limitation. Due to that, Linus Torvalds decided to create a kernel of his own.

It took some time before Linux was released to the public. Linux was released under the GNU General Public License. Due to that, it easily gained popularity towards students, hobbyists, and some organizations such as NASA.

Volunteers and hobbyists did most of the developments of Linux. Most of the applications and components within Linux were initially based from MINIX. However, GNU applications replaced them. That happened because GNU applications were much better and fully and freely available to use — thanks to the GNU GPL license.

The Linux operating system grew fast to the point that many organizations and individuals were able to create separate distributions or flavors of Linux. A few of the most popular Linux distributions are Red Hat, SUSE Linux, and Linux Mint.

On the other hand, when Linux was released many computer retailers and manufacturers such as Dell, IBM, and HP, offered their computers with Linux operating systems installed in order to lessen the control of Microsoft over the operating system market.

Despite being a UNIX offspring, Linux became one of the biggest competitors of UNIX based systems. If Microsoft Windows became

UNIX's biggest rival when it comes to personal computing, Linux distributions became UNIX's biggest rivals when it comes to industrial and web computing.

Linux has been used in supercomputers and embedded systems. Aside from that, they are primarily used in web servers — an industry that was once monopolized by UNIX operating systems. As of this writing, eight out of ten web servers use Linux as their operating system — primarily because of the popularity of the LAMP (Linux, Apache, MySQL, PHP) stack in web hosting.

Direct Comparison between UNIX systems and Linux

Despite having the same roots, UNIX based systems and Linux distros have diverging paths. And most of their differences made and broke some people's preferences over which one to choose. Below are their core differences and similarities.

Pricing and Support

This is where it primarily started. The biggest issue that people have with UNIX based systems is their price. And as discussed a while ago, this is the exact reason Windows have won the operating system market during the 90s.

Unfortunately, pricing issue is nonexistent in Linux. You can download, install, and use Linux without spending a single penny — thanks to the GNU license. However, it does not mean that all Linux distributions are free of charge. Some flavors of Linux are priced. Nevertheless, their cost is much cheaper than Windows and especially much cheaper than UNIX systems.

On the other hand, the price of UNIX systems varies a lot and is much expensive. When it comes to user and developer support, it is part of the package in UNIX. When it comes to Linux support, some distributions offer premium support. But normally, when you are Linux user, you get your support from the community.

User Base

Linux has the widest user base than any other operating systems. It can be as user friendly as Microsoft Windows and Apple OS X, which allows unsophisticated users to enjoy Linux.

Unfortunately, in this aspect, not all Linux distributions are equal. For example, Android OS for smartphones is too friendly for simple users, while distributions for desktops and laptops may or may not be as friendly. It may require some people to get used to the desktop environment of some distributions. Though it is possible to customize a Linux system's interface and change it to a friendlier one such as KDE, GNOME, Cinnamon, Xfce, or Unity. However, it still requires some understanding on how Linux works.

On the other hand, Linux can be as intricate and powerful for industrial applications. High end users such as system admins and program developers enjoy Linux because of its versatility and its readiness to be used in the development scene. A standard installation of Linux can allow people to build a web server within minutes and develop programs immediately thanks to the programming languages and web server application such as Apache they come preinstalled with.

When it comes to UNIX, it is mostly geared towards high end users. It is inevitable since most UNIX systems are created for workstations, servers, and mainframes. If OS X will be included in the mix, it is the only UNIX system (together with iOS) that is useable by unsophisticated users.

Distribution and Development

Linux is free and open source. It means that the development of Linux operating systems is mostly dependent on its community. If a distro's community is helpful, bugs, viruses, and other operating system issues will be immediately reported and resolved. However, if a distro's community is not well managed and helpful, the distro might die.

Of course, aside from problems, upgrade and improvements is also reliant on the user base community. Features and requests are heard out and implemented. In most cases, the community itself will provide the features themselves and offer it to other members.

When it comes to distribution, Linux systems are easily rolled out. Installation package can be downloaded instantly and there is no need for payment. Thanks to Linux's license, it can be distributed and installed in any number of system units without any problems.

On the other hand, vendors handle UNIX systems. Development is continuous and consistent. Fortunately, companies that oversee the UNIX systems are major players in the computing industry, and they are Oracle, IBM, Hewlett Packard, and Apple.

Devices and Usage

Compared to UNIX, Linux can be found in multiple devices and platforms such as watches, smartphones, cars, supercomputers, game consoles, web servers, desktops, and laptops. On the other hand, UNIX operating systems are mostly for smartphones, tablet, watches, workstations, personal computers, and internet servers. However, the big problem is that most UNIX operating systems are shipped together with an OEM device. For example, iOS are available only on Apple products.

Security, Issue Detection and Resolution, and Program Development

Unlike Microsoft Windows, UNIX based operating systems and Linux are secured when it comes to viruses and wares. Both families of operating systems only have more than 100 viruses that can infect them. And most of those viruses are already out of circulation.

When it comes to issue detection, Linux has a clear advantage. First, Linux has a wide user base. If there is an underlying bug in the operating system, it will have a higher chance of being discovered because of the large number of users. Aside from the number of users that might post and notice the problems, Linux also have a large pool of people that can help fix the issue.

UNIX: Operating System Success in a Day

On the other hand, since UNIX is proprietary and does not have a massive user base (except for OS X), issue discovery and resolution might take a while. However, the good thing about UNIX or proprietary operating systems, the development of the operating system is continuous. Even if no one reports an issue, an undiscovered has a higher chance of being addressed even before people knew it was there. Also, UNIX systems take pride of being stable and problem free.

When it comes to program development, there is a slight disadvantage to Linux. Since the market share for Linux is relatively small, most programmers or development teams do not create programs for Linux. And this is especially true when it comes to games.

It has been a common notion that if you are using Linux, you need to be the one to create your program. However, it does not need to be like that. Nowadays, Linux has a large pool of programs and applications. Nonetheless, one should not expect that they will get high quality programs — after all, most them are free and were created by other hobbyists. But things get different if it is about Android. UNIX based systems (except for OS X) also suffer this kind of dilemma.

Chapter 6: UNIX for Developers

In some computer science or programming development courses, it is common that you will find UNIX related courses. As mainly talked about a few chapters ago, UNIX is one of the game changers in the computing industry. And without it, it might be possible that people are still stuck with operating systems that suck balls. And surely, the internet might be not around yet.

But why do program developers need to learn UNIX or be at least familiar with it? Well, there are many lessons to learn in UNIX. UNIX itself will teach programmers how to take advantage of creating modular programs. While UNIX developers will teach programmers how to program efficiently.

The UNIX Philosophy

One of the developers of UNIX, Ken Thompson, created a simple set of rules to follow when creating programs. The gist of the rules is simple — programs must be simple, short, readable, and modular.

As time went by, UNIX developers followed this set of rules. It evolved until it was called the UNIX philosophy. The rules became more detailed. And despite being created decades ago, the UNIX philosophy was still applicable to program development up to this day. The UNIX philosophy adheres or is similar to KISS principle (Keep It Short and Simple or Keep It Simple, Stupid) of literature writing or composing.

Some Companies Use UNIX

This one is a clincher. Most tech companies, especially old ones, still use UNIX. Of course, if you are going to apply for a clerical position, you might not need to learn UNIX. But if you are aiming to be an IT guy, systems admin, or an in house developer, you need to learn UNIX.

However, you do not really need to master it most of the time. In most cases, all you need to do is to become familiar with UNIX's scripting or command shell. On the other hand, if you are going to enter a UNIX centered company, you must also know how the operating system works in the kernel level. If you want to experience UNIX first hand, you might want to try Solaris, Plan9, or OpenBSD (a free UNIX operating system).

UNIX Is Widely Used in the World

As mentioned a while ago, UNIX is the most used operating system in the world (including Linux and OS X). And as of now, the program development industry is focused on creating mobile apps for Android and iOS. If you want to jumpstart your career, it is best that you are familiar of UNIX. After all, iOS and Android are based on it.

The Web Primarily Uses UNIX/Linux

LAMP stack is the way to go when creating a website. Aside from the performance aspect, LAMP servers are much cheaper and easier to use. If you want proof, you can just check web-hosting sites. Most of them have cheaper LAMP than WAMP.

According to a recent survey of W3Techs, 35.9% of the surveyed web servers use Linux, 32.3% use Microsoft Windows, 0.95% use BSD (Berkeley Software Distribution UNIX), and 30.9% unknown operating systems. And it is expected that the data for Linux is underestimated and the data for Microsoft Windows is overestimated.

On the other hand, 95% of mainframes used by Fortune 1000 companies run on IBM's z/OS, Linux on System z, and OpenSolaris for System z (all of them are UNIX based operating systems). When it comes to supercomputers, Linux dominates. Almost more than 95% of all supercomputers use Linux. Only 1~2% of them use UNIX.

Windows

The only time that it is acceptable to not learn UNIX is when you plan on focusing on creating programs on Microsoft Windows. However, it does not mean that knowledge about UNIX will be useless to you if that is the case. Remember that the UNIX philosophy is almost universally applicable in the world of program development.

Part 2: Using UNIX

Chapter 7: Opening a Program on UNIX

Now that you are aware of how UNIX was developed, it is not time for you to understand how UNIX operates.

Unlike other operating systems, UNIX keeps and sorts data and information in forms of files. When you use UNIX, you are required to create new files, rename some of them, replicate copies of important files for storage, remove files that have already served their purpose, search for a file that may have been misplaced in your catalogue system, and print the information stored within the file.

To understand how UNIX manages to do all these task upon your bidding, it is important for you to know what Graphical User Interfaces (GUIs) are. GUIs (pronounced like "gooey") are considered by many as a big leap from merely having to type commands. When using GUIs, you are using your keyboard to type and your mouse or touchpad to point, scroll and click.

A GUI is an interface that combines a graphics screen which features a combination of text and images, a mouse which can be used to point and click, and a system that can divide the screen of your interface into several workable windows to show many programs at the same time.

The GUIs are almost the same as it was more than two decades ago when the very first GUI was released by Xerox. The details and design are definitely different but the system is generally the same.

UNIX Gets a GUI Make-over

It is not a secret that since UNIX is among the first operating system to have been widely-produced for either personal or commercial use, UNIX does not operate using screens. In fact, the very first machine operated by UNIX is a loud terminal that emits loud rattling sounds that prints on actual paper.

UNIX: Operating System Success in a Day

If you chance upon Boston, the Computer Museum has preserved these loud machines. The same can be found in the world-renowned Smithsonian Museum in Washington D.C.

As years went by, UNIX finally appeared to be backing machines that have screens. Most notable of these machines is that of Sun workstations. As an offshoot of the popularity of UNIX, several Window projects from different universities arose. Massachusetts Institute of Technology (MIT) developed the X Windows project which was deemed by many as the successor of Stanford's W Windows project.

X Windows became widely-available and free for anyone who might need it. As a result, almost all UNIX systems operating using a GUI are heavily-founded upon the X Windows system. Some of the many advantages of using X Windows are:

1. MIT gives it away for free.

2. The system uses a webbed client-server architecture that produces different on-screen display depending on the network where the computers are connected.

3. The system is policy independent which means that the screen is not constrained by policies by specific clients unlike Macintosh or Microsoft.

X Windows was designed to work with various computer networks. It introduces a clear difference between a client program, which is the program that does all the dirty computation and evaluation work, and the server program which controls whatever is displayed in the screen. The server program also handles the input data transmitted by the mouse and keyboard.

While these two programs work hand in hand to make UNIX work on a GUI, they are often separately controlled by X Windows. The system divides the workload of controlling the different elements on-screen into three (3) distinct programs:

1. Clients

These programs do the dirty work after receiving input data from the user.

2. Window manager

These programs control whatever appears on-screen. It is responsible for the appearance of windows and manages basic screen functions like resizing the windows, moving the windows to other storage utilities, closing the windows or expanding icons into windows.

3. X server

This program collects input data from mouse and keyboard and transmits them to clients. It also draws the picture (representative of the input data from the user and output data from the client) that can be seen on-screen.

For any given screen, there are multiple clients, one (but can be more depending on the system set-up) window manager and exactly one X server. Each client communicates with the server by giving instructions on what to appear on the screen based on your input data from the same server. Also, the server tells the window manager when the user wants to move the windows or other similar basic window functions.

Although it is more common that all three programs run on the same computer, X Windows makes it possible for these programs to be run by separate machines connected by a single network. It is not uncommon to have a set-up that has clients scattered in different terminals bound by a single network, a server installed on an X Windows terminal and a separate window manager on an adjacent work terminal.

Usually, the Window manager is a UNIX program. If you decide that you don't like how your interface looks, you can switch from one window manager to another. Clients can instruct the X Windows server to perform operations that are more specialized.

Coding an X Windows programs normally takes a great deal of time and effort. In order to expedite the process, programmers often subscribe to coding templates where existing codes are written. They only need to tweak and change certain variables to get the program to perform.

Window Manager Tricks

Before we get to the nitty-gritty like opening files and directories in UNIX, which will be discussed in the succeeding chapters, it is important for you to learn to know how to use the Window Manager to your advantage. Good examples of Window Managers are Motif, CDE and GNOME. For the purpose of this section, we will be using Motif (being the most common Window Manager used by UNIX users.)

Opening a New Window

When you run a Windows X program, it is an obvious requisite that you open a new Window. In order to tell a program that you need to open a new window to reach a specific program, you can use the following GUI-oriented way:

1. Move the pointer (cursor) so that is nowhere near inside your current window.

2. Click the Menu button. This option is the right-most button when using OpenLook.

3. Using your mouse, drag the pointer through the menu list that pops up. Find the program that you want to access.

4. Once you find the program, let go off the button.

The alternative to the steps listed above is a seamless two-step way to open a new window is by:

1. Access a terminal window.

2. Type the file name of the program you want to run.

Using Icons

One of the things that GUIs introduced is the use of pictures as icons. The tiny pictures that are representative of programs or files are scattered in the screen to give you quicker access to them.

When you double-click an icon, the window, which contains the file represented by the icon, pops out. X Windows also allows you to reduce programs to icon so that you are able to access them on a later time.

Wrangling Window design

One of the upsides of using Motif is its seamless design. Every window that you can see on the screen is designed to include a border around it. The border allows users to have control over the window. The border enables users to resize, hide, move and perform various tasks on the window.

Here are other things that you can do with Motif:

1. Change the layering

    This enables the user to switch from one window to another and decide which one is on top of the other. Consider shuffling of papers, you decide that one paper is on top of the other. The active window is usually in front or on top of the whole pile of windows.

2. Manipulate the window size

    Depending on how you want to go about your project or programs, you can change the size of the windows to create either larger areas for long files or smaller areas if you want a subsequent window opened next to it.

3. Move the windows around the screen.

    This is similar to moving around paper around your desktop.

UNIX and CDE

If you have used other Windows computers or even a Macintosh then you would know what a desktop is. In case you still don't know what a desktop is, it is the interface has sleek graphics and clickable icons and menus covering the entire computer screen.

Unlike Motif, the desktop has other ways to organize your files to help you perform your work seamlessly and efficiently. CDE allows you to open different windows and choose between them by merely clicking a mouse. This window manager allows you to drag your files around and share them with programs that can read them.

Chapter 8: Opening Files and Directories on UNIX

Just to give you a refresher, a file is a collection of information kept together in a database, which you can access anytime. In order to keep things organized, every file requires a name to represent it. By the time that you are accustomed to UNIX, you will have hundreds, perhaps even thousands, stored in your terminal.

In order to view the list of files you have on your database, you can type `ls` on a command terminal. (Do not forget to press Enter, which signals that you have entered the entirety of a command line.)

This command stands for "list" so that it will list all the files from the active directory. The ls command lists the filenames in alphabetical order. For instance:

```
budget20       clientli      mail/           springte
12             st/                           rm
                             news.jun
budget20       dan           k               summerte
13ddraft                                     rm
               fallterm      paolo
```

In many Unix systems, directories comprise subdirectories which appears in different colors. Subdirectories are noted by a slash after the name. The succeeding chapters will discuss directories extensively.

Long Form Listing

If you want to view the pertinent information about your files, you can use the `-l` option or long form listing. Type the following on a command terminal:

```
ls -l
```

Please take not that it's not a negative one (-1), it's the letter l. This option will require the computer useful information about a file so that the list will look like this:

```
budget2    1    mdeleon    users      45    Apr  29
      08:57

dan        2    mdeleon    admin     100    Jul  14
      15:57

fallterm   3    mdeleon    users     229    Sep  16
      02:45

mail/      4    mdeleon    users    1189    Mar  12
      19:08

paolo      5    mdeleon    users    1328    Mar  10
      10:10
```

The first column shows the file name. The second column shows the number it appears on the list. The third column shows the author. The fourth column shows the users who have access to the file. The fifth column shows the size of the file in terms of the number of characters. The sixth, seventh and eight columns show the month, day and time the file was last modified respectively.

Making and Showing Hidden Files

There are times where you need to hide files to prevent other people from accessing them. UNIX enables you to show these hidden files that do not appear in the ls listing. In order to make a hidden file all you have to do is affix a period (.) to the filename. For instance, if you want to hide a file named formyeyesonly, you can type:

```
.formyeyesonly
```

UNIX will then hide your file from plain view. If you want to access your hidden files, type:

```
ls -a
```

Subsequently, if you want to display all pertinent information about your hidden files, you can type:

```
ls -al
```

As you may have noticed, this command merely combined -a and -l commands to display a long version of the list of file names. This is the same as:

```
ls -a -l
```

which obviously required you to type an extra space, character and punctuation. UNIX will then give you a list that looks like this:

```
.summer    1      mdeleon    users      29    Dec   5
        04:58

.budget2   2      mdeleon    users      405   Nov   19
        10:47

.apollo    3      mdeleon    admin      1028  May   8
        12:30

.dane      4      mdeleon    admin      100   Apr   1
        18:27

.google/   5      mdeleon    users      19    Sep   14
        25:18
```

Copying and Duplicating a File

In order to make a duplicate copy of a file, you must remember the exact name of the file you want to copy. Also, you are required to name the duplicate differently. For instance if you want to follow the format of a file named springterm.2012 to make another similar file (which you will name springterm.2013), you can type:

```
cp springterm.2012 springterm.2013
```

Make sure to leave spaces between the command `cp`, the original file and the new file. This command gets the contents from `sprinterm.2012` and creates an exact copy with under a new name: `sprinterm.2013`.

The command `cp` is used to copy a file by creating a new file that has a new name but with the exact same contents.

Warning: Do Not Lose Your Work

Unlike newer Operating systems, UNIX does not warn you when you are overwriting a file that has an identical filename. For instance if you already have an existing file names `springterm.2013`, it will be replaced with the contents of `springterm.2012` after using the `cp` command in the previous section.

It is important, therefore, to use the `ls` command first to make sure that there is no similarly-named file.

In more recent versions of UNIX, however, the `-i` option allows you to instruct `cp` to inform you whenever you are overwriting a file or when a name is already taken. If the filename is already taken, the `-i` option will inquire if you want to proceed with duplicating a copy of the original file to an already-used filename.

Instead of just `cp`, you can use this nifty feature by typing `cp -i`. Consider the following:

```
cp -i sprinterm.2012 springterm.2013
```

If it doesn't return any message, then there's no existing file with the same name.

Rules on Filenames

UNIX has four rules on naming files; they are:

1. UNIX is case-sensitive. This means that they consider uppercase and lowercase letters as different letters. For instance:

    ```
    Springte          springTE          SpRiNgTe
    rm                RM                Rm
    SPRINGTE          SPRINGte
    RM                rm
    springte          sPrInGtE
    rm                rM
    ```

    are all different filenames as far as UNIX is concerned.

2. Do not put spaces in filenames. While other programs allow users to put spaces in filenames, spaces only cause trouble because a select few programs does not accept them. Instead of space, use periods or underscores.

    Refrain from:

    ```
    Springterm 2013
    ```

    Instead, use:

    ```
    Sprinterm.2013 or Sprinterm_2013
    ```

3. Do not use weird characters when naming a UNIX file name, they might have special uses for UNIX that might interfere with the system. As much as possible stay away from:

    ```
    `       \\      *       <       >
    ^       !       /       {       }
    #       |       &       [       ]
    $       ?       ~       (       )
    ```

    Try to stick to just number and letters.

4. UNIX allows 14 characters but newer version have larger limit in the number of characters in the file name. For instance:

```
A_filename_can_be_this_long_or_thiiiiiiiiii
iis_long
```

is a valid filename.

Deleting Files

UNIX allows you to remove or delete files that you no longer need. For example, if you no longer have use for `Springterm.2012`, you can type:

```
rm Springterm.2012
```

To check whether the file has been removed or not, use the `ls` command. Also, be warned that there is almost no way to recover a file once it is deleted. To be on the safe side, you can use the `-i` command to program UNIX to ask for further confirmation before you delete a file. Type:

```
rm -i Springterm.2012
```

UNIX will then ask:

```
rm: remove `Springterm.2012'?
```

Press y on your keyboard to confirm deletion or n if you want to cancel deletion.

Deleting files should be done for the following reasons:

1. It is confusing to have different files stored in your computer especially if these file are not properly sorted.

2. Useless files take up portions of your computer's memory. The UNIX system might have problem processing your data

if you don't remove unnecessary files and free up space from your disk.

It is a good idea to make extra copies of important files to make sure that you have copies whenever you make revisions.

Rename Files

Suppose that you want to change the filename because of various reasons like it being a typo error, you can replace its name by using the mv command. For instance, you have a file called: Srpingterm.2013 and you want to change it to `Sprinterm.2013`. You can correct the filename by typing:

```
mv Srpingterm.2013 Springterm.2013
```

Just like when using the `cp` command, renaming a file with an already-used filename changes the contents of the filename with the contents of the previous filename.

In order to prevent unintentional file clobbering use `-i` to tell UNIX to require a secondary confirmation that you want to rename the file. Also, you can use a period to prefix the filename of a file you want hidden.

For instance:

```
mv -i Srpingterm.2013 Springterm.2013
```

The Contents of a File

Two (2) main kinds of UNIX files exist:

1. Files that have special codes that can't be translated when displayed on-screen. These types include program files, database files, spreadsheet files and other kinds of files.

2. Files that only have text that can be appropriately displayed on-screen. These are text files.

Displaying the Text Files

In order to display the contents of the text files, type `cat`, which means catenate or catalog. For instance, of you want to open a file named `Springterm.2013`; type:

```
cat Springterm.2013
```

If the file is long, and you only need to see the first ten (10) lines of the file, you can use the head command. For instance:

```
head Springterm.2013
```

only displays the first ten lines of the code.

Permissions

Unlike most of the operating systems, UNIX was built to be used by more than one user. The system has devised a way to track who the owner of the file is and what other users can do with it. These permissions can come in three forms:

1. Read-Only Permission

   This form of permission allows users to open the file and read it. It also allows you to copy the file, which only produces another read-only file.

2. Write-Only Permission

   This form of permission allows users to edit the file. Even if you are allowed to edit or change the file, there's no way for you rename or delete it. If you are given a Write-Only permission in a directory, you are allowed to create new files and delete files from it.

3. Execute Permission

   This form of permission does not only allow you to read or write, it allows you to execute the permission. If the file does not involve a program file then an Execute permission is useless.

There is a way to know which groups you belong to and thus what kind of permissions you are given. To do this, type:

```
id
```

UNIX will display something like this:

```
uid=149(dan)                    gid=102(admin)
groups=224(admin)
```

This means, user named `dan` is an `admin` and belongs to the `admin` group. Whatever permissions provided to the admin group can be enjoyed by user `dan`.

Determining the File

UNIX has a way of telling you the type of file is stored in its directory. It uses special characters.

1. Directory, File or Symbolic Link

UNIX tells you which category it belongs to by the first character in a name.

– (hyphen)	file
l	symbolic link
d	directory

2. Read, Write or Execute (owner)
Unix tells the owner if she can read, write or execute a file by the next three characters in the line.

r	read
w	write
x	execute

-         in place of r,w,e if you can't read, write or execute.

3. Read, Write or Execute (group)

Unix tells you whether the group can read, write or execute a file by the succeeding three characters in the line.

r	read
w	write
x	execute
–	in place of r,w,e if you can't read, write

or execute.

4. Read, Write or Execute (others)

UNIX tells you whether other users can read, write or execute a file by the last three characters in the line.

Gather the above information by typing:

```
ls -l Springterm.2013
```

which displays a detailed listing:

```
-rwxrw-r--
```

Break down the above output into:

-     which means that the `Springterm.2013` is a file
r   which means the owner can read `Springterm.2013`
w   which means the owner can write `Springterm.2013`
x   which means the owner can execute `Springterm.2013`
r   which means the owner's group can read `Springterm.2013`
w   which means the owner's group can write `Springterm.2013`

\-   which means the owner's group can't execute
`Springterm.2013`
r   which means others can read `Springterm.2013`
\-   which means others can't write `Springterm.2013`
\-   which means others can't execute `Springterm.2013`
Permissions can also be expressed by UNIX to a three-digit
number. If this is the case then:

First Digit	Owner's permission
Second Digit	Group's permission
Third Digit	Other people's permission

The digits are numbered from 0 to 7, each with their own
corresponding permission levels:

Digit	Permission Level
7	Read, write and execute
6	Read and write
5	Read and execute
4	Read only
3	Write and execute
2	Write only
1	Execute only
0	None

This means that if UNIX said the file is 741, then it means
that

7	The owner can read, write and execute the file.
4	The group can only read the file.
1	Others can only execute the file.

Changing Permission Levels

UNIX: Operating System Success in a Day

In order to change the permission type for a certain user or group, you can use a combination of letter and symbols composed of the following

1. The group or individuals whom you are changing permissions.

u	user or file owner
g	group
o	others
a	all three

2. Whether the permission should be turned off or on

+	on, yes
-	off, no

3. The permission you want to turn on or off

r	read
w	write
x	execute

For instance if you want to change permissions for the filename `Springterm.2013`, type the following:

```
chmod     a+r Springterm.2013
```

This command line means that you want to turn on the read permission for the owner, group and other users. Consider the following example:

```
chmod uo-e Springterm.2013
```

This command line means that you want to turn off the execute permission for both the user and others. Using the digit matrix in the previous page, you can also set the permissions by:

```
chmod 770 Springterm.2013
```

This means you are allowing both the owner and the group to have read, write and execute permissions while leaving none for other users.

Changing File Ownership

If you want to change the owner of a file, you can type the following:

```
chown mdeleon Springterm.2013
```

This means you are changing the owner of the file named `Springterm.2013` to a user named `mdeleon`. Others can also replicate the file first before changing the name of the new file.

Directory

In order to organize the files in folders, UNIX allows users to create directories and subdirectories so they can divide them in different groups. This portion will explain how you can categorize files into different directories.

If you are Windows users, here are the following bits of information that you should know:

1. The backslash (\) that Windows users are used to becomes ordinary slashes (/) in UNIX.
2. UNIX changes directory is similar to DOS Window's `CD` command only that UNIX requires that you use lowercase letters `cd`.
3. When making a directory, you can't use `MD` as in DOS Windows. Instead, the command for making directory is `mkdir`. When removing a directory, you can't use `RD` as in DOS Windows. Instead, the command for removing directory is `rmdir`. Never capitalize both UNIX commands.

4. Just keep in mind that UNIX differentiates lowercase and uppercase letters so just make sure to use lowercase when using UNIX commands.

Directories are UNIX's version of Window's and Mac's folder. UNIX requires the users to christen directories with a name. For instance, a directory named /TermExams directory can contain other subdirectories like /SpringTerm, /FallTerm. These subdirectories can also contain further subdirectories like /FallTerm.2012, /FallTerm.2013, /FallTerm.2014 and /FallTerm2015. The subdirectory /FallTerm2015 can contain FallTermMidTerm.2015 and FallTermFinal.2015.

Here is how these can be viewed in a tree-structured directory:

in Directory	Subdirectory 1	Subdirectory2	Files
rmExams	/SpringTerm	/SpringTerm.2012	
	SpringTermMidTerm.2012		
	SpringTermFinals.2012		
		/SpringTerm.2013	
	SpringTermMidTerm.2013		
	SpringTermFinals.2013		
		/SpringTerm.2014	
	SpringTermMidTerm.2014		
	SpringTermFinals.2014		
		/SpringTerm.2015	
	SpringTermMidTerm.2015		
	SpringTermFinals.2015		
	/FallTerm	/FallTerm.2012	
	FallTermMidTerm.2012		

```
FallTermFinals.2012

                          /FallTerm.2013
FallTermMidTerm.2013

FallTermFinals.2013

                          /FallTerm.2014
FallTermMidTerm.2014

FallTermFinals.2014

                          /FallTerm.2015
FallTermMidTerm.2015

FallTermFinals.2015
```

Naming Directories

The rules for naming directories are the same with naming files. Funky and unconventional characters must be avoided. Some programmers use capitalization to distinguish filenames from directory names to tell which are which.

When using UNIX, the current directory that you are working on is referred to as the working directory. Upon logging in, the home directory is considered the working directory. If you transfer to the /TermExams directory, it then becomes the working directory.

If you forget where the current file is in the directory structure, UNIX can tell you where. Just type the following command line:

```
pwd
```

This command is an abbreviation for print working directory. It does not print the details on paper; instead, the details are displayed on the screen. For instance, if you are in /FallTerm.2015, the screen will display:

```
/TermExams/FallTerm/FallTerm.2015
```

Every time you use the ls command, UNIX will just list the files from the working directory.

If you want to access a different directory aside from the /FallTerm.2015 directory, you can type:

```
cd /SpringTerm
```

to go to the /SpringTerm directory. There are two ways to tell UNIX which directory you want to access. They are:

a. Key in a relative pathname. (Relative pathname are the pathnames from where you are currently.)

   Ex. SpringTerm

b. Key in the absolute pathname or the full pathname. (Full pathnames are the pathnames that enumerates the roots until the designated subdirectory where your file belongs to.)

   Ex. /TermExams/SpringTerm

If you try to go to an inexistent directory or if you were not able to type the name of the directory correctly, UNIX will display:

```
SrpingTerm: No such file or directory.
```

Note that the example provided above used the misspelled version of /SpringTerm to highlight that /SrpingTerm does not exist.

When you want to go back to the home directory, UNIX only requires you to input this command:

```
cd
```

UNIX assumes that you want to go to the home directory if you don't specify the landing directory when using the `cd` command.

Making Directories

Whenever you are creating new directories, it is important to make sure that you are in the right place. In order to display the directory that you are working at currently, type:

```
pwd
```

The most common place where people make directories is their home directory. In order to get there type:

```
cd
```

Just like when creating files, you christen a directory with a name that will represent the contents. For instance, if you want to create a temporary holding directory for your files you can create a `Temp` subdirectory. In order to create a `Temp` directory, key in this command line:

```
mkdir Temp
```

Many people create a Temp directory to hold their temporary files. These files are stored in a temporary directory for a variety of reasons. These files are kept only until they are printed or copied to an external device. After making the `Temp` directory, proceed by checking whether the directory exists by typing:

```
ls
```

Another way to check if the new directory exists is by proceeding directly to it. Do this check by:

```
cd Temp
ls
```

All directories are created empty until you save files to it. Here are the common examples of directories:

1. Documents
This is where people often store important documents, letters or memos.

2. EMail
This is where people often store electronic mails from bosses.

3. Temp
This is where people often store files they don't plan on keeping on a long-term basis. This also separates the more important files from the less important files.

4. Trash
This serves as the central location for files that are no longer needed.

Transferring Files

One of the handy things that you can do with a UNIX file is being able to transfer files from one directory to another If, for example, after looking through the list of files, you decided that you wanted to transfer a file from one directory to another to keep your files organized and free from clutter. This task can be accomplished by using the mv command.

In order to use the mv command effectively, you must know two (2) things:

1. Name of the file that you need to move; and
2. Name of the directory where you need the file to be moved.

UNIX also allows you to rename the file as you move it. For instance, you have a file named:

```
SpringTermFinals.2015
```

and it belongs to the directory named:

```
/TermExams/SpringTerm/SpringTerm.2014
```

instead of:

```
/TermExams/SpringTerm/SpringTerm.2015
```

The best way to move the file from one directory to another is to locate the directory where the file is originally located. To do this, type:

```
cd /TermExams/SpringTerm/SpringTerm.2014
```

After UNIX brought you to the designated directory, use the `ls` command to locate the file you want to transfer. Once you are sure that the file is indeed inside the directory, you can start transferring the file by typing this command line:

```
mv SpringTermFinals.2015
/TermExams/SpringTerm/SpringTerm.2015
```

Take note of the space between the command `mv`, the filename `SpringTermFinals.2015` and the destination directory `/TermExams/SpringTerm/SpringTerm.2015`. To make sure that the file is no longer within the `/TermExams/SpringTerm/SpringTerm.2014` directory, you can use the ls command. To check if the file was moved to the destination directory, proceed to the said directory and ran the ls command again.

As a rule of thumb, always check your command line before you hit Enter to make sure that you have coded your command to match the instructions or tasks you have in mind. Be careful because there's a chance that if you just mistyped a couple of letters, you will be sending an important file in an obscure directory.

Removing Directories

When removing directories, you can easily use the command `rmdir` but for this command to work safely, you are required to first move or remove the files inside the directory. To delete a directory successfully, you may follow these steps:

1. Using what you have learned from the previous sections, remove the files that you don't need.
2. If you still need some of the files, make sure to move these files to other directories using the mv command.
3. After emptying the directory, move to a different directory.
4. Delete the directory by keying in this command line:

   ```
   rmdir FileToBeDeleted
   ```

5. To make sure that the directory no longer exists, you can use the ls command.

Although it's easier to delete parent directories to weed out its subdirectories but doing so can lose you important files that may have been stored in one of the subdirectories.

Renaming Directories

Unlike DOS Windows, UNIX allows users to rename directories after creating it. This is made possible by the handy mv command.

When renaming a directory, you need to tell the command the original directory name before the new directory name. Proceed to the parent directory of the directory that needs to be renamed. For instance, if you want to rename /SchoolWork to /Assignments, you should first go to the parent directory. Once you reached the parent directory, you can key in this line:

```
mv SchoolWork Assignment
```

Again, it is important that the new directory name is not being used by a different directory. Otherwise, the contents of the original directory will be wiped out and replaced by the contents of the directory whose name was changed.

Popular Preexisting Directories

Directory Name	What's in It?
/bin	This directory contains the usual system commands.
/usr/bin	This directory contains standard commands used by users.
/usr/contrib/bin	This directory contains commands that are more specific; those that are distributed third-party platform.
/usr/local/bin	This directory contains installed system codes that are often not part of the standard directory.
/dev	This directory connects devices like drivers. They seldom contain any files. (One of the good things about UNIX is how they are able to trick its system to treat hardware devices as if they were also files.
/etc	Other files that the system use to work effectively and efficiently.
/home	This contains the home directory for UNIX

	users. Aside from `/home`, the home directory can also be accessed with `/usr/home`
`/lib`	This contains codes and commands that are vital for some programs to run.
`/usr/lib`	This contains more specialized commands and codes that the programs use to perform well.
`/tmp`	This contains less-specific temporary files.
`/usr/tmp`	This contains more specific, and usually larger, temporary files.
`/usr/src`	This contains the source code of the whole system.
`/var/src`	This is a different place where the source code is stored.
`/usr/man` and `/usr/catman`	This contains a database of the UNIX manual.

Printing in System V

For users who are using the UNIX System V you can print our output by using the `lp` command. For instance if you want to print the content of `SpringTermMidTerms.2015`, you can type this command line:

```
lp SpringTermMidTerms.2015
```

UNIX will then respond with the following information:

```
request id is md-2334 (1 file)
```

This means that UNIX is processing the file that you want printed.

Printing in BSD UNIX

For users who are using the BSD UNIX, you will need to use the command `lpr` instead. For instance:

```
lpr SpringTermMidTerms.2015
```

will print the same output as that of in the previous section's example.

Chapter 9: Useful UNIX Utilities

Now that you have learned the basics of how to use the facilities of UNIX, this chapter will then discuss the best utilities from this Operating System. After learning several nifty commands discussed in this chapter, you will find them handy once you start using UNIX extensively.

Comparing Files

Sometimes after replicating a file, you will find it hard to check the difference between the two without opening the file. UNIX has two commands that can aid you in this endeavor. These commands are: diff and cmp.

The command cmp is a simple comparison program that determines whether two files contain the same content or not. For instance, when comparing these two files, type:

```
cmp                         FallTermMidterms.2015
FallTermMidterms.2014
```

This will check whether there were changes done from the 2014 file. Regardless of content, cmp can compare any kind of file. All it cares is to determine whether the files are identical to each other or not.

Aside from cmp, UNIX also takes pride in the diff command. This program will not only tell you if two files are different but will tell you how different they are. The only difference is that diff can only cross-check text files. The only downside of this program is that it can't process other documents including word processor documents.

For instance, when comparing FallTermMidterms.2015 and FallTermMidterms.2014, you can type:

```
diff                        FallTermMidterms.2015
FallTermMidterms.2014
```

After entering the two file names, the `diff` program will respond by displaying this output:

```
5c5

<This is your MidTerm Exam for Academic Year
2015-2016.

—

>This is your MidTerm Exam for Academic Year
2014-2015.
```

This means that the main difference between the two files can be found on the fifth line as highlighted by `5c5` in the output. `5c5` means that diff program compares the fifth lines of both files and takes note of their differences.

Sorting Files

One of the handy functions of computers is being able to sort a very wide range of files and arrange it an order that you desire it to. Unlike its predecessors, UNIX introduced a very nifty sorting program that organizes files.

The command `sort` has a variety of uses that you may find useful. For instance, if you want the contents or lines inside files to be arranged alphabetically as is in a list, you can use the `sort` command to perform such function.

One of the nifty characteristic of the sort program is its creation of a different file to protect the integrity of the original file in case the sort program does not give your desired result. For instance if a file named `ClassList.2015` contains a list of students enrolled in a class, you can have the list arranged alphabetically in a new file called `SortedClassList.2015` by typing this command line:

```
sort ClassList.2015 > SortedClassList.2015
```

If you are confident that the sort program won't mess up your list, you can sort the contents a file without making a new file by typing this command line:

```
sort ClassList.2015 -o ClassList.2015
```

This way, the sorted contents of `ClassList.2015` designates itself as its own output file as per the `-o` command option. If you try to use

```
sort ClassList.2015 > ClassList.2015
```

you will only end up with your file wiped out because the above command line first clears the destination file of its contents before it is filled with the sorted contents of the original file. That being said, you should be careful when naming your destination file as the filename might already be taken.

Also, the sort command uses a strict comparison between internal ASCII codes that UNIX use as a database for text hence it sorts numbers and letters in a correct way. One problem that persists, however, the uppercase are sorted before lowercase letters. For instance, when sorting a file named `Alphabet.List` that includes the following:

```
ZETA
alpha
CORAZON
flora
beta
```

The sort command will arrange the lines to show:
```
CORAZON
ZETA
alpha
beta
flora
```

In order to negate this effect, you can use the command −f (fold cases) to sort the list regardless of the case. For instance, if you type this command line

```
sort -f     Alphabet.List -o Alphabet.List
```

the output file will display:

```
alpha
beta
CORAZON
flora
ZETA
```

There are other options that you can use when sorting data. Each of them uses a different command to instruct UNIX how to sort out data.

−b   This tells UNIX not to mind the spaces at the beginnir line.

−d   This tells UNIX to sort lines the way dictionary sorts w usually ignores any punctuation marks. This is often use −f command.

−n   This tells UNIX to sort lines based on the number that each line. This makes a list where 99 is followed by 100 a to the other way around as in the alphabetical order.

−r   This tells UNIX to sort lines in a reverse order. This fur be combined with the rest.

Date and Time

UNIX systems have programmed clocks within it. Users can even ask UNIX to provide the exact date and time by using the date command:

```
Date
```

The system will then respond by supplying this information:

```
Tue Jun 4 20:23:49 EST 2015
```

Also if in case you want to tell UNIX to carry out a specific task at a specific future time, you can use the `at` command. For example:

```
at 23:01pm Jun 4
sort        -n        ClassList.2015        -o
UpdatedClassList.2015
    pr -f -2 UpdatedClassList.2015 | lp
```

If you are contented with the above instruction, press Ctrl + D on your keyboard to indicate that you finished encoding the command. By 11:04 pm of June 4, UNIX will sort the contents of the `ClassList.2015` file by number and input the sorted version inside the `UpdatedClassList.2015` file. Afterwards, it prints the resulting file.

Determining File Contents

There will come a time when your directories will be brimming with so many files rendering you unable to remember what is inside each of them. The good thing about UNIX is that it has a nifty `file` command that gives you a hint at the contents of each file.

For instance, if you are working on a directory named `/SpringTerm.2015`, you can type:

```
file *
```

UNIX will then display an output that may seem, at first, to be incomprehensible information like:

```
SpringTermMidTerm.2015:    Microsoft    Office
Document
    SpringTermFinals.2015: ascii text.
```

In other words, it displays what type of content each of the files has.

Part 3: UNIX And The Internet

Chapter 10: Web Surfing for UNIX Users

As mentioned in the first Unit, UNIX was built and designed to work on a multiple-user system. It is therefore not surprising that while UNIX may have been an old Operating System, UNIX users can still access the internet and work with the network as efficiently and effectively as modern systems these days.

In the interest of security, you can determine who has been using your computer. There are three ways to make sure that you have safe access to the internet and that no one has tampered with your terminal to mine data and hack your information. These ways are: (a) who, (b) w, and (c) finger.

When you type in the who command, UNIX will respond something similar to this:

```
mdeleon     console          Jun   12    10:58
mdeleon     ttyp1            Jun   13    11:58
Andy14      ttyp2            Jun   14    12:45
mdeleon     ttyp3            Jun   14    09:58
mdeleon     ttyp4            Jun   15    17:22
mdeleon     ttyp5            Jun   16    10:55
```

If you are for instance, mdeleon, this means that a user named Andy14 accessed your terminal on June 14.

A more detailed output is displayed by finger command. Consider this output for instance:

Login	Name Office	Type	Idle	Login	Time
mdeleon	Marlon De Leon 10:58 NY	console	2d	Jun	12
mdeleon	Marlon De Leon 11:58 NY	ttyp1	1d1h	Jun	13

y14	Andy Bradford	ttyp2	5d	Jun	14
	12:45	SF			
leon	Marlon De Leon	ttyp3	9h	Jun	14
	09:58	NY			
leon	Marlon De Leon	ttyp4	12:30	Jun	15
	17:22	NY			
leon	Marlon De Leon	ttyp5	4h	Jun	16
	10:55	NY			

If for instance, you want to know more about Andy Bradford, you can use the finger command to know more about him. Type in the following information:

>finger Andy14

UNIX will then respond with the following display:

```
Login: Andy14                        Name:       Andy
Bradford
Directory: /home/Andy14              Shell:
/bin/slash
Office: San Francisco, 789 745 6856
On since Sat Jun 13 12:45 (EDT) on ttyp1, idle 4
days
Project: ClassList.2015
```

Browsers

When connecting to the World Wide Web, you use a browser to perform various tasks in the internet. There are different kinds of browsers you can use to gain access to the information stored in the internet. These include Rockmelt, Chrome, Mozilla, Opera and Conqueror to name a few.

When using UNIX, you can either type the name of the browser installed (this requires installation and is not included in the system by default) in your system to open the browser. Usually, when using

UNIX shell, you can click on graphical icons that represent the browsers.

Browsing in UNIX does not differ a lot from you might have been browsing the net using a different system.

Going through different sites:

1. Click on the Location input box located at the top portion of the browser.

2. Type the URL of the website you need to access. Often, you don't have to include the http:// portion of the URL.

3. Press Enter on your keyboard.

Getting Files from the Net

UNIX has a unique way to get files from the internet. The requisite in performing this task is to run the ftp program and to get connected in the server. For instance:

ftp ftp.mde.com

For the sake of this example, we will be accessing mdeleon's computer that has an ftp address of ftp.mde.com. If you are able to access the ftp network successfully, the server will display a message that reads:

```
Connected to ftp.mde.com
    20  tom.mde.com  FTP  server  (BSDI  Version
6.00LS) ready.
```

In order to copy a file from the FTP server located in the internet, you can use the get command. For instance, you want to copy a file named InternetFile, you can type:

```
Get InternetFile
```

Conclusion

Thank you again for purchasing this book!

I hope this book was able to help you understand UNIX.

After knowing the basic details about the UNIX operating system, you should go ahead and start exploring it. You have multiple options for you to get familiarized with UNIX. You can start with fiddling your smartphone or try working with your Linux or OS X computer.

And in case that you want to experience UNIX first hand, you can download and try using OpenBSD. Fundamentally, you will not be lost if you already have experience when it comes to handling Linux systems. On the other hand, if the only operating systems you have used before are Microsoft Windows or Apple OS X, expect that you will take some time before you get used to UNIX.

Finally, if you enjoyed this book, please take the time to share your thoughts and post a review on Amazon. It'd be greatly appreciated!

Thank you and good luck!

Below you'll find some of my other popular books that are popular on Amazon and Kindle as well. Simply click on the links below to check them out. Alternatively, you can visit my author page on Amazon to see other work done by me.

C Programming Success in a Day

Android Programming in a Day

C ++ Programming Success in a Day

Python Programming in a Day

PHP Programming Professional Made Easy

CSS Programming Professional Made Easy

Windows 8 Tips for Beginners

If the links do not work, for whatever reason, you can simply search for these titles on the Amazon website to find them.

Lightning Source UK Ltd.
Milton Keynes UK
UKHW012047050123
414908UK00011B/157/J